My State LOUISIANA

By Christina Earley

TABLE OF CONTENTS

A Crabtree Seedlings Book

Crabtree Publishing

crabtreebooks.com

School-to-Home Support for Caregivers and Teachers

This book helps children grow by letting them practice reading. Here are a few guiding questions to help the reader build his or her comprehension skills. Possible answers appear in red.

Before Reading:

- What do I know about Louisiana?
    - *I know that Louisiana is a state.*
    - *I know that Louisiana has swamps.*

- What do I want to learn about Louisiana?
    - *I want to learn which famous people were born in Louisiana.*
    - *I want to learn what the state flag looks like.*

During Reading:

- What have I learned so far?
    - *I have learned that Baton Rouge is the state capital of Louisiana.*
    - *I have learned that Mardi Gras is celebrated with parades.*

- I wonder why...
    - *I wonder why the state flower is the magnolia.*
    - *I wonder why there are ruins at Fort Macomb.*

After Reading:

- What did I learn about Louisiana?
    - *I have learned that you can canoe along Bayou Teche.*
    - *I have learned that the state animal is the black bear.*

- Read the book again and look for the glossary words.
    - *I see the word **capital** on page 6, and the word **ruins** on page 16. The other glossary words are found on pages 22 and 23.*

LOUISIANA
Hi! My name is Zoey. Welcome to Louisiana!

I live in Breaux Bridge. It is the **crawfish** capital of the world!

There is a festival with music and food every year in my city.

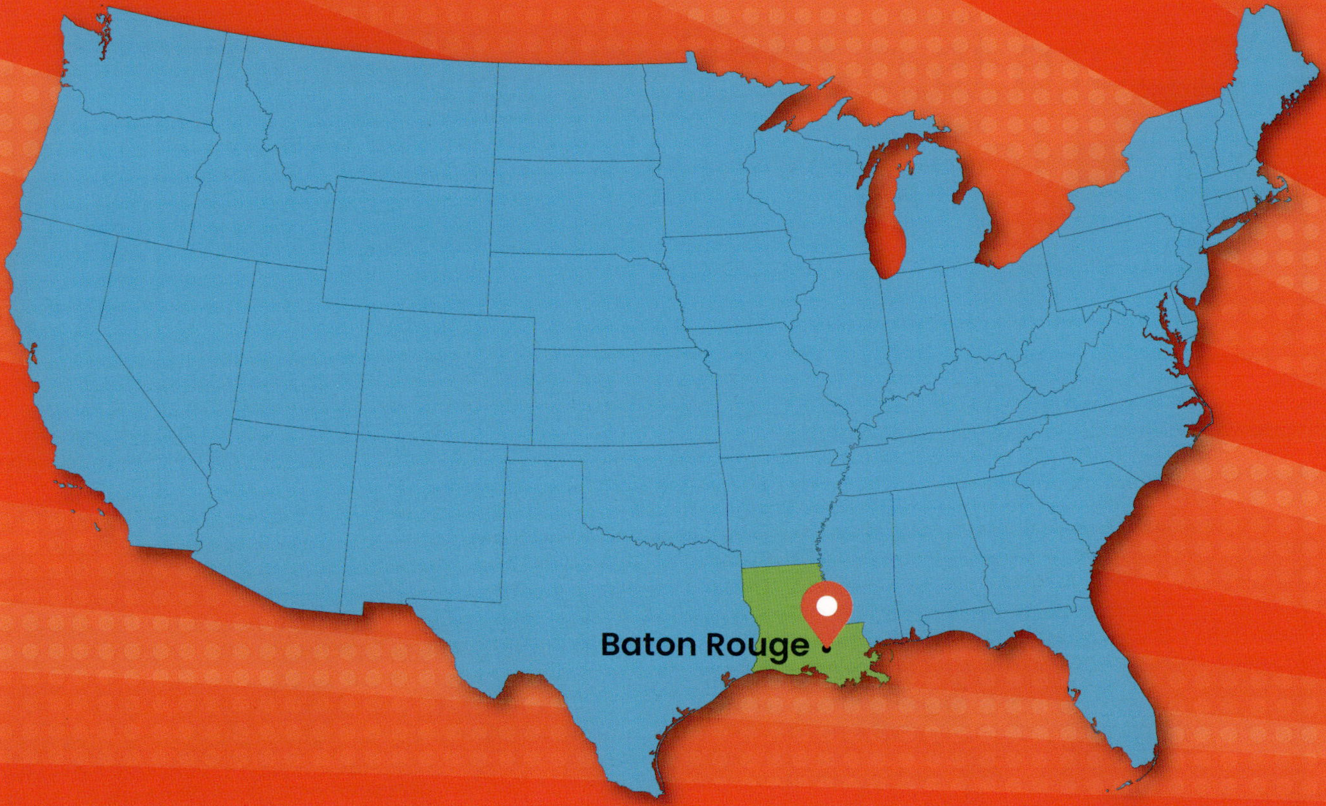

Louisiana is in the southeastern United States. The **capital** is Baton Rouge.

Fun Fact: New Orleans is the largest city in Louisiana.

The state animal is the black bear.

The magnolia is the state flower.

We grow a lot of sugarcane in Louisiana. Some of it is used to make powdered sugar for **beignets**.

Fun Fact: Louisiana **produces** 13 million tons (11.8 million metric tons) of sugarcane a year.

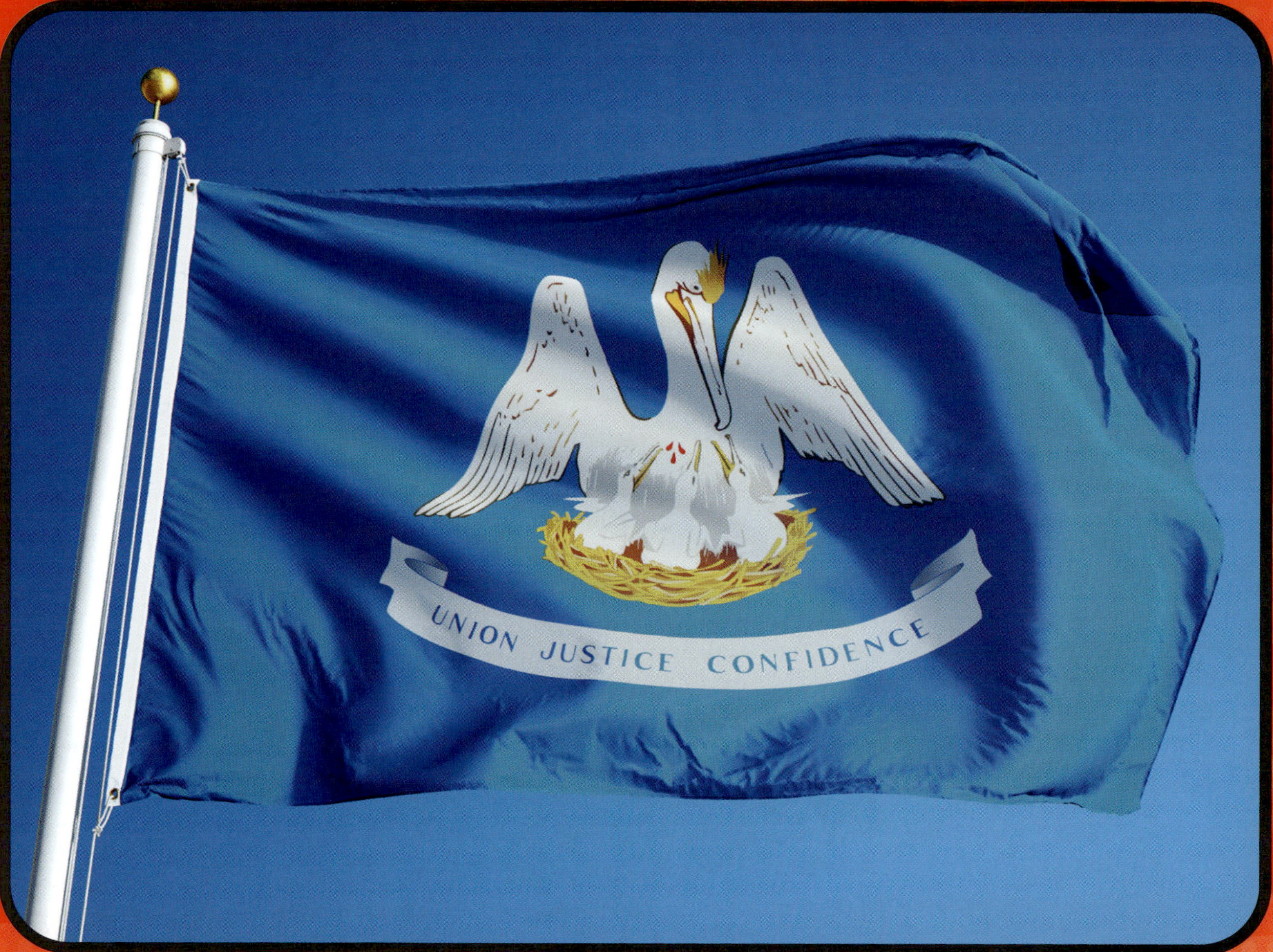

My state flag is blue. There are pelicans in the middle.

There are two national sports teams in Louisiana.

We celebrate Mardi Gras every year with parades. The floats have many colors.

Fun Fact: The official colors of Mardi Gras are purple, gold, and green.

REX

I like to learn about our history at the **ruins** in Fort Macomb.

I enjoy riding the Ferris wheel at Carousel Gardens Amusement Park.

Trumpeter Louis Armstrong was born in Louisiana. NFL legend Peyton Manning was also born in Louisiana.

Fun Fact: Madam C.J. Walker, the first African American female millionaire, was born in Delta, Louisiana.

My family and I canoe along **Bayou** Teche.